EVO

The Evolution of a Woman

By
Chimere Bacon-Destin

Co-Authored by the Real Housewives of Houston

2021

Copyright © 2021 by Chimere Bacon-Destin

All rights reserved. This book or any portion thereof may not be reproduced or used in any manner whatsoever without the express written permission of the publisher except for the use of brief quotations in a book review or scholarly journal.

First Printing: 2021

ISBN 978-1-7379629-0-8

Ordering Information:

Special discounts are available on quantity purchases by corporations, associations, educators, and others. For details, contact the publisher at the above-listed address.

U.S. trade bookstores and wholesalers: Please contact rhwohinfo@gmail.com

DEDICATION

This book is dedicated to the women
that I encountered Evolution with
My Grandmother (In Legacy) -"Alva Merlene Bacon"
My Mother - "Alva Jimerle Bacon"
My Aunts- Verona "Kay Kay" Bacon | Demetria Bacon Grimble
My Nanny (In Legacy) - Rhonda Thompson
My Best Friend (Lifelong) – Roxie McLeod
My Best Friend (In Legacy) - Monique Lusk
My Future - (My Daughters) - Channya TaNise Watson
Jasmyn Ssky Moffett | Cyncere Sereniti Moffett
And last but not least all the women who have supported, and been
a part of our organization
"The Real Housewives of Houston"

TABLE OF CONTENTS

DEDICATION	iv
LIST OF AUTHORS IN CHAPTER ORDER	1
ε	2
FIREFLY	3
GOLDEN OPPORTUNITIES	9
MY BLOOD-STAINED BANNER! HIS BLOOD FREED ME!	16
GRACEFULLY REFINED	19
RESILIENT WOMAN	26
WINNING WOMAN WARRIOR	32
BALANCE QUEEN	36
ν	41
WOMAN REVEALED	42
A STORM THE WHOLE TIME	46
WOMAN WARRIOR	56
RISING PHOENIX	63
DEBORAH	70
AMEREPIPHANY	76
ο	82
MEET THE REAL HOUSEWIVES OF HOUSTON	83
ABOUT THE LEAD AUTHOR	91

LIST OF AUTHORS IN CHAPTER ORDER

1. Vaneasa Harrison
2. Sabrina Golden
3. Channell Dawson
4. Roxie McLeod
5. Jaie Williams
6. Delcine Thomas
7. Tiffany Monroe
8. Vanda Smith
9. iiiYansaje T. Muse
10. Cadori
11. LaShawn Watson
12. Tricia Kyle
13. Chimere Bacon-Destin

Ε

In the beginning, no, this is not the bible, but I guarantee the beginning stories of each of these women will learn you something. Hello World, Chimere here, and I gathered a few of my beautiful sisters to tell their story about how they have evolved as a woman.

We thought it would be good to share our stories, because the true testimonies may encourage you to move, shift, and press. When you think about Evolution, you think about change in the most invasive notion. How do we evolve, how do we change, how do we become the best versions of ourselves?

The "E" is for Everything
Everything you have encountered
Everything you have gone through
Everything you wanted to do
Everything you are doing now
Everything you thought you were
Everything you are growing to be
Everything they called you
Everything you said
Everything you receive
Everything you give
Everything you allow
Everything you give into the atmosphere
Everything you've learned
Everything-

FIREFLY

Vaneasa Harrison

Evolution is inevitable for every person. The way I see it, the experiences and choices we make determine who we will evolve into.

When I was a child, I spake as a child, I understood as a child, I thought as a child: but when I became a man [woman], I put away childish things. —1 Cor. 13:11

Growing up in Livingston—a small town north of Houston—taught me a lot, and I'm so thankful for it. My parents are pillars of the community. They always have their hands on a worthy project, so I look up to them in admiration.

Our family had a grocery store, Bob's One Stop, on the West End in one of the few black neighborhoods in Livingston. It was across the street from the old Dunbar High School, where only 'colored' kids attended school. When I was five, my brothers and I would run around the store and eat as much candy as we could without getting in trouble. My mother, who was always vigilant about our antics, made sure that we were full of beans and cornbread. That way, we wouldn't eat from the store and cut into the profits.

I never thought about if we were poor or not, and my parents celebrated and defended everything we had. This taught us that every step forward is a monumental occasion. When my mom gave me my own room and saved money to decorate it with Rainbow Brite, it was a huge deal. It was the most beautiful thing I had ever seen! Everything was Rainbow Brite: the bedspread, the pillows, the curtains. I even had the Rainbow Brite doll and her unicorn sidekick, Starlite.

One day, a little neighborhood girl around my age showed up at the store playing with a Rainbow Brite doll. I felt devastated because I knew for certain that it was mine, but she insisted that it was hers and wouldn't give it back. When I told my mom, she was angrier than I was.

"Oh, you're going to get your doll back today," she declared as she held my hand and marched me up to the girl's yard.

She instructed me to tell the girl to come out with the doll, and I did, scared and all. When she came out, the girl shouted, "This is my doll! My mama bought it for me." My mom knew that it was no coincidence that she had a new specialty doll at the same time that mine came up missing.

That day, my mom, who was usually an amicable woman, cheered me on as I fist fought for my doll! I hit that girl as hard as I could. I was out of breath and a little confused but happy to have my doll back, and my mom was proud of me. Afterward, she told me, "You can't just let people take your stuff right in front of your face, 'cause they'll do it if you let them."

My mother, Daisy Harrison, has always been a huge influence in my life. The way that she evolved in front of my eyes has given me the power to know that I can too. We all need a role model to follow, a woman who can show you how to grow, and she was mine.

My mom's journey with reading reveals her eagerness to evolve. When she recognized that she couldn't read very well, she pushed herself to improve. She picked up a book and started reading until she came across a word that she didn't understand. Knowing that the word looked familiar, she stared at it but could not make sense of it. After mulling over the word, she laughed at herself when she realized that the word was jump. "How on earth," she would say, "did I graduate when I can't even read the word jump?"

It wasn't long until our walls were full of posters with information about learning to read. My siblings and I took part in making the posters and discussing our thoughts with each other. Our mom told us that we would have to contribute to our own education because we couldn't rely on somebody else to do it. She knew that having strong reading skills would benefit us no matter what we decided to do with our lives. Her decision to improve herself and to share that growth with us is something that will stick with me for the rest of my life.

By the time I got to high school, I could talk your ear off. I was an avid reader and participated in many school clubs. I performed well in academics, sports, band, and cheerleading—I felt like I could change the world. I'm so thankful for the support that I had from my family and friends. Even though it wasn't perfect all the time, I felt good about life.

Pep rally days were exhilarating! We cheerleaders would get The Livingston Lions pumped up for the game that night. The whole school would gather in the gym along with family, friends, and community members.

On the day of a pep rally, my friend, Rey, came to me and exclaimed, "Vaneasa, you're the perfect person!"

"The perfect person for what?" I wondered.

"I have a friend, Manny. He's new here. Can you help me show him around? You know, show him how we do things around here?"

"Yeah, I can help," I shrugged.

Rey introduced us. Manny and I happened to have a class together, so, as we made it to our seats, I explained to him why today was the perfect day to start school in Livingston. With classes shortened because of the pep rally, he could go to the football game tonight! He was quiet, so I probed him to see what kind of kid I was dealing with. He nodded yes to everything, even if it wasn't a yes or no question. Weird.

Then he muttered, "No hablo inglés."

I knew it meant something in Spanish. When I figured out the translation, I exclaimed, "Oh! You don't speak English!" After congratulating myself on my Spanish skills, a realization hit me like a ton of bricks. Wait, what? We can't understand each other! How did Rey think I was going to help? We're not even speaking the same language! Despite my disbelief, I promised that I would help him.

That's when things got interesting. I had never listened to anyone so intently in my entire life. I focused on every sound that he made and repeated his words back to myself. My Spanish classes were more engaging because I actually had a purpose for learning the language. Every day, we spoke to each other in broken Spanish and English. We did our best to communicate and laughed at our mistakes as we struggled. Good times. We learned a lot from each other.

I will always cherish my friendship with Manny even though we haven't spoken in a while. Sometimes it only takes a moment to change the trajectory of life. Everybody experiences those pivotal moments. You've had them too if you think about it, right? They are the times that we tell our kids and grandkids about.

The lessons I learned from a determined mother and my experiences with Manny are gifts I will pass down to my children. Looking into my daughter's eyes for the first time, I was completely overwhelmed by the reality of it. Her eyes...there was something profoundly beautiful about looking into the eyes of my first-born daughter.

I was in labor for five days before her delivery. The days leading up to her birth were full of uncertainty, but I kept my faith in Almighty God as my creator and sustainer. As a woman with a vivid imagination, I could not fathom how this enormous bundle of joy could pass through me.

For years, I have seen how my parents work as a team to build their businesses and raise a family. Even though it isn't perfect, they communicate and have family meetings when somebody feels like they need to share their feelings. When I visit them, I sometimes find notes that my mom has written to my dad about their life, love, or struggles. In a way, their relationship gave me an expectation for my own family. Unfortunately, my family's dynamic didn't turn out the same, and the disappointment of it almost cost me my life.

My interest in Spanish continued to grow, and eventually, I received the honor of induction into the Spanish Honor Society. Upon graduation, I received a Spanish scholarship from Sam Houston State University—where I was fortunate enough to work as a student-teacher.

Setting off for college, people thought that I was capable of so much, but it didn't take long for me to realize this next level was much more demanding than high school. Indeed, I made mistakes and got caught in the pitfalls that my elders had warned me about. Even with my issues and getting into some unproductive activities— I was still learning. Thankfully, I ended up pulling myself together.

Soon after I recovered from my slump, I created a program to help people learn English or Spanish and boost their careers. Through this program, I took a trip to Costa Rica where I saw the Arenal Volcano erupt. I gazed in awe as the lava lit up the night sky and drizzled down, reminding me of how small I am at the mercy of God.

My experience in Costa Rica endowed me with my spiritual name, Cielo, meaning sky or heavens. My soul reaches out towards the heights of the Almighty God, and I'm humbled by His omnipotence, humbled by my interactions with His people—made after His image, humbled by my shortcomings in the grand scheme of my assignment on this earth, humbled by my femininity, and humbled by my continual evolution.

ABOUT THE AUTHOR:
Social Media:
IG @harrisonvaneasa
FB @vaneasa.harrison
Website Address vaneasaharrison.com
Email vaneasaharrison@gmail.com

Vaneasa Harrison is a spiritually anchored woman who is a mother, teacher, strategist, and entrepreneur ~passionate about helping people catapult from potential into next level mastery. Currently, she is a bilingual teacher who instructs students in all subject areas. She has been teaching, at the elementary level, since 2007, in grades ranging from Pre-kindergarten to fourth grade. She conducts language projects to assist highly motivated adults to learn the English or Spanish needed in their careers. She has taught financial literacy in schools and cities across the nation assisting future heirs and millionaires to solidify their financial systems. Harrison uses proven techniques to coach individuals to live their best life in a dynamic and effective way.

Did you know that most people don't become wealthy because they don't take the time to study the language of wealth? Yes, wealth has its own language, and it can be learned by anyone.

Are you interested in participating in one of our language projects?

Book a consultation today.

GOLDEN OPPORTUNITIES

Sabrina Golden

Growing up in a single-parent Asian home was a good thing for me. I learned so many things, such as how to respect my elders and how not to ruin my name or embarrass the family. I learned how to serve and respect others and many other things that I still do and teach my children to do as well. I was a watcher, so I would watch people's outcomes and make decisions based on them. For instance, I saw how much it hurt when a person's partner cheated on him or her. So, I vowed never to bring that pain upon someone. To this day, I value my family's traditions, which few people appreciate nowadays.

These values and morals made me the person I am today. Along the way, though, you learn a lot more. I strive to make the most of my life and to be the best because I value my name and how others perceive it. I want to leave this life knowing I have had an impact on people's lives, leaving a legacy.

My purpose is to be a light in this dark world. Knowing that we all go through something, I never want to make a person feel worse.

Instead, I would rather be that glimpse of hope and light that makes them feel at ease and peace.

When others disagree, I try my best to please and love everyone and not choose sides. I state what is right and love both people back to righteousness. Sometimes that practice can interfere with my goals. Which makes others perceive me as a pushover or try to take advantage of me. But it's what I am built for. In the end, both people will know I was there for them and loved them the whole way through with no malicious intent. No one will make me go to hell for unforgiveness. While I may get hurt and angry for a minute, I do not hold grudges.

My mother was my mother and my father. She raised me by herself at a time of heavy racism. She fought to raise a half-Black child and went through many ordeals. Her own Chinese people shunned her, but she did what she had to do with no education and did a great job if I say so myself. She sheltered me, but she also taught and warned me. She used the things she went through to show me what could happen if I did things wrong.

My mother is the strongest and most influential woman I know. She has instilled in me values and morals that are hard to come by. She has been my greatest rock and supporter. Even though we may not see eye to eye, she is the best mother, doing the best she can. I appreciate all that she has sacrificed for me. She showed me that in life, you can travel and eat all the good foods and have nice things. Yet you also need to be humble about it. No matter what, you stay humble. Rich or poor, beautiful or ugly—never hold your head too high.

I grew up shy. When my mother introduced me to people, I would hide behind her. I didn't talk much unless I got to know a person. Then I sometimes became a chatterbox. Boisterous friends helped bring out the crazy, fun side of me. They also spoke up for me. I still have people like that in my life. They know I won't speak up unless I need to address something. Otherwise, I like my peace and keeping people happy. Even if I have to discuss something unpleasant, I speak in a non-hurtful way. That is, I do unless someone has pushed me to a boiling point, which rarely happens.

Growing up, I generally stayed on the straight and narrow. My mother sheltered me and I was naïve to a lot of things. As a tomboy, I played basketball and powder-puff football. Every year, I made touchdowns and interceptions in powder puff, which awarded me the MVP award my senior year.

Early in life, I had many long-term relationships. I had two boyfriends, got involved with other men during the same time, and then got married. While single, I had breakfast, lunch, dinner, and late, late dinner dates on some days. My mother went crazy thinking I had sex with each man. That wasn't true because most men didn't make it past the date. As a parent now, I understand why my mother worried, but having been so sheltered, I got excited to be around people. As an only child having fun with people and seeing them smile gives me joy. I love seeing people happy and laughing, enjoying themselves.

Married at the young age of nineteen and starting a family six months later, I learned to grow up fast. For eighteen years, I dealt with an abusive and adulterous husband. Because my heart holds so much compassion and love, I took him back after every betrayal. Yet he would only do it again. People asked me all the time why I stayed so long.

"Because," I say, "when I was young, my father was not there. So, I made a promise to myself that I would fight to make sure my kids had their dad."

Thus, I stayed, hoping and praying things would get better. Maybe my husband would stop and appreciate whom he had by his side. But he never realized it until after I left.

When I decided to get a divorce, I prayed and asked God if it was okay to do this.

The Spirit said, "I gave you the release after the last affair, and you stayed."

I thought, "Man, you are so right."

However, I was pregnant and had no job. So, I stayed, especially because every time I tried leaving, my husband would take away the car and money. He controlled what I could do and not do.

With these manipulative types of people, you tell yourself, "Oh, this time it will be different. This time, he will change."

Then the person deceives you again with his or her smooth words and actions.

My husband was good with words and even mentioned to me, "If it's a Black woman, I can talk her into anything."

It never dawned on me what he meant. Until I started reminiscing and writing my memoirs (this book will come out soon).

While growing up, I did not attend church. But then I came to Houston, started going to church, got saved, and learned more about God for myself. Also, because my husband was the son of a pastor, I had a lot of the Word instilled in me. Still, I had a rude awakening when I became part of that family and learned more about the characters of people. It made me open my eyes because I trusted everyone and everything (and still do, but now I try to be more cautious). I value my character, so I never wanted to mess my name up by cheating on my spouse or doing something else I regret.

My breaking point came when I finally got tired of my husband and his last woman beating me down. I don't discount anything I went through, because it has kept me grounded and brought me to my evolution moment. At that moment, I realized I needed to do me and be a light in this dark world. With so much hate, backbiting, malicious intent, and cold-heartedness in people. I do not want to bring any child of God down.

My epiphany happened when I opened my eyes to my worth and began to develop self-love. Like a lightbulb moment, several truths all flashed before me. I was worth more than others taking advantage of my kindness and forgiveness. My kids should not believe that a husband could treat his wife this way. My girls should not believe that they should accept this kind of treatment from a man. My children needed to see me make it through life by myself, with no man's help.

I had always told my husband that I would never cheat on him. If I decided to, I said, I would file for divorce and never come back. And I did as I said I would. My husband thought I would forgive him yet again after his last betrayal. Getting the divorce papers shocked him. Then he lied even more and did some mean things. He knew that once I had made up my mind to divorce him, I would not turn back.

I love keeping my word; if I can't, then I will let you know. But I went against my morals by seeing other men before my divorce became final. Though I knew these other men wanted to lock me down as soon as I got out of my marriage, I was not ready. This time, I know what I want in a husband and will not settle for anyone who can't take the challenge on. This time, I need to see if I can please a new man and vice versa. If not, we are not getting married. I do not believe in divorce except in cases of physical abuse and adultery. Everything else, we need to work on.

My ex-husband's affairs made me the strong woman I am today. Now I like to analyze myself and see both sides of everything. I look at what I can do different and how a situation could have gone better so I can try to improve myself. From this relationship, I also learned that you have to find your inner peace and self-love to be happy. You cannot expect a man or woman to fill your voids. Find your purpose in life. When you do, you will walk with confidence, happiness, and prosperity.

After my divorce, I did a retreat to get some healing and open my eyes to things I had missed or too deep-rooted issues. Sometimes we do not know that we react the way we do because of these deep-rooted things. This retreat, called BARE, helped me to see and a spiritual cleanse. I felt free after it. Still, I don't want you to think that everything went away after that. As I had to, you have to work on seeing, cleansing, and being mindful daily. I encourage all women to go and cleanse their spirits.

Even with all that my ex-husband did, I still forgive him. That does not mean I would take him back, but it means I let God deal with him so I can have peace of mind. We all have unique pitfalls. Mine is forgiving people when I shouldn't or still loving on people who have done me wrong. For example, sometimes people ask why I hang out with this person or that person. I do it because I try to love everyone with no judgment.

We all have done something wrong. Some mean to, and some don't, but we all have to take responsibility for our actions at the end of the day. I do not want to be part of someone's fall or envy, and I do not want to hate on anyone's joy or happiness. No, I will have my own peace, love, and happiness.

Evolving into the woman I am today is the most fulfilling and joyous feeling in the world. Knowing my purpose and walking in it has brought me to people, places, and things I never thought I would reach. From being a shy girl, I have grown into hosting TV talk shows, branding, and running my own business.

I couldn't ask for anything more. One of my main goals is to lay my head down at night knowing I have no malicious intent toward anyone. I live my life free and clear. I know what God has promised me, and He has not let His child down.

ABOUT THE AUTHOR:

Social Media:
IG @GoldenOpportunitiesHouston
FB @ReporterSabrinaGolden
Email brinaskelton@aol.com

Sabrina Golden is a single mother of three children, whom she loves with all her heart. She is a model, actress, media personality, MUA, and entrepreneur. Sabrina co-hosts the TV show Boss Up Houston. In her segment "Golden Opportunities," she highlights entrepreneurs. She gives them a chance to shine. Golden has worked with stylists and designers such as Tim Thorn and Diannetta Chargois. Also, with Markina Smith, Alexandria Lee Designs, Kameereo Crisp, and many more. She has worked in and on the runway and high fashion. Golden worked in print, editorial, commercials, plays, movies, and shorts. She owns S Golden Strategies, a company that offers social-media maintenance. The company offers coordinating, consulting, connecting, and more. In her spare time, she loves volunteering and attending church. While working on many other projects.

MY BLOOD-STAINED BANNER! HIS BLOOD FREED ME!

Channell Dawson

As a child, I always dreamed of a white house with a picket fence, a tall chocolate husband, and some little chocolate babies, but God had other plans. Morally, what stuck with me was that I would do whatever it took to prove the doubters wrong in every aspect of my life. As a wife, mother, daughter, sister, and friend, I am doing just that.

The most influential women in my life are my mother, Maxine Maiden-Webster, and my mother-in-law, Denise M. Hosenbackez. Watching my mother push through every challenge, obstacle, setback, and delay to ensure that my siblings had what we needed to survive is one of the most memorable qualities that have molded me into who I am today. When I met my husband's mother, I realized that she had many of the same qualities as my mother, and that is a double blessing to me.

I faced many obstacles while growing up, but I struggled most with mental health and learning disabilities. If not for my willingness to submit to the word of God, I would still be lost in the world or six feet under.

I struggled with certain morals. I lied when the truth would have done just as well. I lacked confidence and had low self-esteem. I envied other women because I had just as many qualifications as they did but never had the tenacity to accomplish what they did. The Holy Spirit and my relationship with God, my husband, my children, and my family brought me back to a point of comfort.

I've learned that we can achieve anything in life, especially when we have the willingness to do it and the mindset to master and overcome the obstacles that stand in the way.

My evolution moment came when I realized that God had a bigger and better plan for me than the world around me had to offer.

The Holy Spirit and the whispers of God's voice drove me to my spiritual name. They said, "Daughter, I know the plans I have for you ([Jeremiah 29:11, NIV]). Come from among the chickens and soar with the eagles, and I will never leave you nor forsake you. Your family will be blessed; your husband will be blessed; everyone down to your children's children will be blessed. Everyone you speak over will be blessed. If I give you a word, it will not return to Me void, but it will accomplish what I put it in you to do ([Isaiah 55:11, NIV].

My breaking point occurred when I saw that everyone around me would be blessed, but I still struggled with surrendering to God on the level that He wanted to use me in. Once I put away my childish thinking and "leveled up" in God, everything began to fall in place faster than I could receive the latest blessing.

I reached an epiphany when I realized that God is a jealous God. He will not share any part of me with the world. I could no longer hop backward and forward or from hot to cold to lukewarm in my life ([Revelation 3:15–16, NIV]). I had to walk in oneness with Christ. Choosing who I would serve is not an 80/20 percent, but rather a 99/1 percent—because Christ Jesus, through God, was the only perfect person to walk in the flesh.

ABOUT THE AUTHOR:
Social Media:
IG @cdawson0425
FB @cdawson0425
Email cdawson0425@gmail.com

Channell Dawson has worked for the federal government for fifteen years. She has held multiple positions, including positions in leadership. She takes pleasure in using her leadership skills to develop other leaders and serves as a powerful force in the workplace and community.

Channell takes inspiration from her husband of eighteen years, her fourteen-year-old daughter, and her two-year-old twin son and daughter. In her free time, Channell enjoys motivational speaking, encouraging leaders to be greater leaders, inspiring underprivileged individuals with avenues to become privileged in their endeavors, and helping undereducated individuals to seek means of higher education for career and life advancement.

Channell has an associate's degree in Christian counseling and eighteen years of experience in marriage, parenting, and career counseling. She also holds multiple licenses, leadership certifications, and life-coaching certifications, including master life coach, mindset coach, and cognitive-behavior coach. At the end of every encounter with individuals or family units, Channell makes it her mission to assist them in living their best lives and proving the doubters wrong.

GRACEFULLY REFINED

Roxie McLeod

When I was five years old, my Mexican mother married a black man. His name was Lemuel Paul Tillman, Jr. I remember looking up at him as he towered over me like the mountains in California. He had beautiful, deep brown skin and straight white teeth that I swear, glowed in the dark. He raised and claimed me as his daughter. One thing's for certain, **he loved me**! Blood couldn't make us any closer. To this day, I believe he was the only man who ever truly loved me unconditionally and I loved him back just the same.

My mothers' family became disappointed in her choice to marry outside of her race and didn't speak to her for a while. My stepfathers' family wasn't too happy about their relationship either. I remember both families did come together for the wedding. My dad's, dad, who I called Mr. Tillman, officiated their wedding. Every Sunday, we attended Mr. Tillman's Pentecostal church. He ended every sermon the same way. By asking the congregation to say with him, Ephesians 4:32, "And be ye kind one to another, tenderhearted, forgiving one another, even as God for Christ's sake hath forgiven you.'" This scripture got ingrained in my soul. Little did I know, it would stick with me and pull me through some really tough times.

The most influential woman in my life is my mother. As a child, my mother would make me stay inside cooking and doing chores while my brothers played outside. The skills that she taught me that I once dreaded, have proven to be the most useful and rewarding. It was her who taught me how to be a wife and serve my husband, how to be a mother and care for my children, how to tend to my house, and how to go out and hustle. She may not be the most graceful; she is a little rough around the edges. She doesn't glide down the street like a dainty, white Porsche. She moves more like an 18-wheeler truck, hauling a trailer! She is a force to be reckoned with, and I strive to be like her every day.

I grew up in Scenic Woods, a small, all-black neighborhood in North East Houston where I believe my mother and I were the only Mexicans. I didn't know what or who I was at that time. I didn't speak Spanish fluently so the Mexican kids didn't accept me. My dad and brothers were black, but the black kids at school didn't accept me either. It took me a while to figure out my own identity and accept myself. My best friends were Chimere and Courtney. Our weekends and summers got filled with cool cups, double dutch, skating tricks, and sassy cheer competitions. Life as I knew it, was simple and fun but also a little confusing.

Trying to find love in all the wrong places, I lost my virginity at the age of fifteen. Those couple minutes of pleasure landed me at Planned Parenthood. It was my first visit to an OBGYN and I'll never forget the discomfort of the cold, metal tool the doctor used to examine me. A week later, my dad opened a letter in the mail from my secret visit to the doctor's office and went absolutely berserk! His little girl was no longer a little girl anymore and she had an STD. That news on top of me already being a defiant teenage girl, he decided to kick me out of the house. I begged and pleaded with them to forgive me and let me stay.

I remember looking over at my mom saying, "You really going to let him kick me out?"

Fed up she turned around and walked away. This is when life got real. Life was no longer simple nor fair and not the least bit fun. It was a major turning point in my life. I went from living in a loving, two-parent home with my three younger brothers. To a rat and roach-infested home on the outskirts of Downtown Houston with my biological father. He was hardly ever home. He spent most of the time at his girlfriend's house because it was closer to his job. He would bring me money for groceries on the weekends and occasionally stay the night after being out bar hopping. There were two occasions that he tried to have sex with me but, thank God, he was unsuccessful. He later apologized and I eventually forgave him. Scared and lonely I kept thinking of the scripture Mr. Tillman made me repeat over and over again. Some days I went to school but most days I didn't. I began smoking cigarettes and drinking alcohol to distract myself from all the pain I had inside. Most of that part of my life is a blur but like Maya Angelou said, "Still I Rise,".

Between the ages of twenty and twenty-eight, I was still searching for a man to love me. My first love was with a man named Real. His real name was Renaldo and he was eleven years older than me. He swept me off my feet. We had an on-again, off-again, friends with benefits, a relationship that lasted for about twelve years.

I had a brief relationship with a man from Ghana who spoke French and had hazel eyes. He was everything a woman could dream about. We lived together for less than a year and planned to get married. Until one day he decided to push me up against the wall during a heated disagreement. I moved out the very next day.

Then there was the radio producer. Oh, my goodness! She shook me to my core. Her presence, her voice, and her passion were irresistible. We lived together in Dallas for a year and then moved to California for her job. We were together for a total of two years, but I knew in my spirit, I wasn't meant for her and she wasn't meant for me. When you love someone the way I loved her, you have to let them go. That's exactly what I ended up doing and then I went back home to Texas.

Then, there was the coach. He was a retired professional football player that played for the Green Bay Packers. We had about a year-long "entanglement", as Jada Picket-Smith would put it. He was so fine and well put together. We met through a cousin of his who was a soldier in the Army. He had a cousin stationed in Spain and was passing through to visit. I had one unforgettable night with him. Don't roll your eyes! You live and you learn.

By the age of twenty-five, I was pregnant by my on-again, off-again, childhood love. You remember, Real? I knew the exact moment that I got pregnant. I'll never forget it. I drove my little two-door sports car down to Huntsville, TX to go pick him up from jail. He had gotten locked up while I was in Cali with the radio producer. He got locked up for about a year, so you can imagine all that built-up aggression. I brought him back to my place and one thing led to another. Twenty-seven weeks later my first child was born prematurely, weighing only three pounds at birth. She has proven to be a fighter and a true blessing from God. Life was no longer about me. It was and still is all about her.

On the night of October 1, 2008, I remember driving on the freeway in my broke down Honda Accord sipping Hennessy and Coke in a styrofoam cup. I had a cigarette in my left hand that I kept dusting off through the crack of the car window. I cried out to God on the way to the club asking Him to save me from myself that night. I got tired of using and all the abuse, and I was ready for a major change. I had no idea where to start, but I knew I would keep getting the same results if I kept doing the same things.

On that same night, I met the man I would marry. I was at a bar with my best friend, Deanna, drinking my pain away. She insisted I go speak to the only black man in the club at the time. It wasn't my style to approach a man so I refused at first. After a few more drinks of liquid courage, I decided to step outside of my comfort zone and go speak to him. He was exactly 6'1" and weighing about 240 pounds or so. He had the prettiest, pearly-white teeth and wore a silky, John Travolta-looking shirt to match his smile. We talked all night long and even into the morning in the parking lot of the club. Four months later, on February 2, 2009, we got married. I'm pretty sure I got pregnant on my wedding night. After ten years of marriage, three strong boys, two years of separation, and lots of ups and downs, we divorced on February 27, 2021.

In those twelve years, I learned how to be a wife and a mother. I quit smoking and drinking, and I learned what I am willing to put up within a spouse and bring to the table myself. I wouldn't change any of it because it allowed me to find out my purpose in life. Although I believe our purpose changes as we grow and evolve, I realized that caring for children was my passion. It was something ingrained in me as a young girl and came so naturally to me as a grown woman. All that time I spent helping my mom cook, clean, and watch my brothers was for a reason unbeknownst to me. Watching my grandmother iron her husbands' shirts for work and make his lunches everyday was all making sense to me now.

I find joy in taking care of children. Not only that but helping other nannies perfect their craft as well. God knew what He was doing all those years. It wasn't by accident or coincidence. Even going through what I went through as a child helped me gain compassion and empathy for other young children. He was molding me all along. If it weren't for all the pain and roadblocks throughout my journey, I wouldn't have the passion that I have for children now. I pray over every child in my care that God covers them with His shield of protection. I also pray He help me the best way I can to ensure they don't deal with the same hardships that I did. My goal is to be a safe, loving adult that they can look up to and learn from.

I am evolving into the woman God has called me to be. Not defined by the shade of my skin or any of my past mistakes. I am a mother, a daughter, a big sister, and an overcomer. I am more than enough. I am Roxie McLeod, fearfully and wonderfully made, and I am willing to share my truth with anyone who can benefit from it. I pray that other women will find comfort and encouragement when they hear or read about my story because we all go through things. In the words of Rocky Balboa:

"It ain't about how hard you hit. It's about how hard you can get hit and keep moving forward."

ABOUT THE AUTHOR:
Social Media:
FB @TheNannyRoxie
Email thenannyroxie@gmail.com

Roxie McLeod is "The Nanny." She has over twelve years of experience in childcare, including working as the lead teacher at two major learning facilities. She has worked with groups of all sizes, ages, and needs but specializes in infant and toddler care. Roxie prides herself on building long-lasting bonds with children and families. She has a Child Development Associate (CDA) credential and extensive CPR training.

Roxie leads other women to develop programs that allow them to make their own schedules and achieve financial stability. She actively participates in the Real Housewives of Houston group, connecting with like-minded women who are making major moves in their businesses, personal growth, and development. She co-hosts the Boss Up Houston Talk Show on Boss Up Houston Network.

In her free time, Roxie enjoys live music, the arts, good food, and time with friends and family, including her four children. If you would like to become a nanny, conduct a nanny share, or get advice, you can reach Nanny Roxie at thenannyroxie@gmail.com or through her Facebook page, "The Nanny Roxie."

RESILIENT WOMAN

JAIE WILLIAMS

Whatever you hold in your mind will tend to occur in your life. If you continue to believe as you have always believed, you will continue to act as you have always acted, and you will get what you have always gotten. If you want different results in your life or your work, all you have to do is change your mind.

—Anonymous

I am the oldest of three siblings. I have always been responsible, and I love hard. What I mean by hard is that there is absolutely nothing I wouldn't do for my family. The women in my life have taught me to be strong and to take care of myself and my siblings no matter what.

My mother is one of seven sisters. She and her siblings are the most glamourous, independent, and intelligent women I know. Because of them, I fell in love with fashion and beauty at a young age as I became mesmerized by their extensive beauty rituals. They would often gather at my Granny's house to get dressed for nights on the town. My cousin and I would sit in the doorway of the restroom, watching them perfect their hair and makeup. Their attention to every detail from top to bottom was impeccable.

I wanted to look and be exactly like them. Not only are they beautiful, strong black women, but they are also all career-driven and successful. They work hard at their careers and play hard on their nights out, but they never stray from their values. They taught me that I can do anything I set my mind to, and they were right! There is nothing I cannot do.

Their beauty provided them with a privilege that I wanted as a child. To my young mind, it seemed like they got whatever they wanted because of their charming glamour. Like them, I am beautiful, and I have inherited the benefits that my mother and aunts have. My beauty has manifested relationships, divine connections, and job opportunities. However, I've learned that being physically beautiful means nothing if you aren't happy, and I was not. I carried anger and pain in my heart, so I acted out.

Marrying at a young age, I became a mother of two children nineteen months later. I married for the wrong reasons; I wanted to get out of my parents' house, I was pregnant, and I had no idea what I was doing. As a young wife and mother, I molded myself into a person that would please the people in my life. Life at some point became miserable and I needed to escape from my marriage, but I didn't until ten years had passed. My fear of the unknown kept me from leaving that relationship.

The divorce process was chaotic. I was afraid to confide in anyone because I assumed that they would encourage me to opt out of the divorce despite my feelings. Later, I realized that seeking counsel is vital when you are dealing with trauma on your own. After the divorce, I realized that I didn't know myself, not even something as simple as what I like or dislike. I lost myself in my marriage by trying to be something I had no business being at the time—a wife. While recovering from that trauma, I had to accept the fact that my younger self's choices led me to failure. Prayer and affirmations guided me through this process of healing and acceptance.

Getting to know myself again taught me that there are several aspects of my happiness that I needed to work on. Not long after realizing this, I met my current husband. Our romance was a whirlwind, and something about him made me want to be his wife. It wasn't until after I had fallen in love with him that I discovered that he was dealing with trauma and depression, but I believed that we could get through anything together. We got married three years later.

Two years into our marriage, we ran into a major obstacle. My husband went to prison for four years. Being alone again was heartbreaking, but I stuck by him every step of the way. I visited him every weekend in an attempt to keep our marriage alive, but, despite my efforts, I started to fall out of love with him.

When my husband returned home, we had to learn about each other all over again. It's been six years, and things are still difficult, but we are committed to making our marriage work. Through this chapter of my life, I realized that I am strong and can persevere through any situation life throws at me. Knowing now that I can take care of myself—the fear of being alone is gone.

Life did not take long to offer up a new challenge; my son's diagnosis of Enlarged Vestibular Aqueduct Syndrome—hearing loss—struck him at the age of eleven. Growing up with the ability to hear then losing it at a gradual rate took a toll on him. Over time, he began isolating himself. As a mother, there is nothing more painful than watching your child struggle with something that you can do nothing about. My son was hoping for a miracle, but his hearing continued to deteriorate. He was depressed and moved out of his father's home in May of 2019, and we have not heard from him since.

To cope with my maternal dread, I pray for my son, asking God for his protection, mercy, grace, and favor. Regardless of what he decides to do with his life, his path is his alone to determine what's best. Whatever he chooses, as a loving parent I will support him—

when he is ready to reach out again. Although this situation has been traumatic, I have learned a lot because of it. I've realized that no matter what decisions you make, good or bad, they are yours alone. All of the accountability falls with the decisionmaker—you.

Despite the obstacles that I've endured, rededicating my life to Christ and immersing myself in His excellence has allowed me to pursue my dreams. This journey has led to the removal of toxic relationships from my life, and God has replaced them with beautiful and genuine relationships. I am grateful.

It is important to surround yourself with people who love you and will support you—no matter what. I have had my fair share of opportunistic relationships, but now, I am only interested in true connections. It's all about choices: the choice to be the best, the choice of pursuing my dreams, the choice of being a loyal and supportive friend.

Favorite Quote/ Bible Verse:
"For I know the plans and thoughts that I have for you, says the Lord, plans for peace and well-being and not for disaster, to give you a future and a hope." (Jeremiah 29:11 NLT).

ABOUT THE AUTHOR:
Social Media:
IG @gorjizz_jaie @allmadeupbyjaie
FB @jaie.williams.9
Email jaiewilliams@live.com

Owner of **All Made Up by Jaie** in Houston, Texas specializing in natural and clean makeup applications for the everyday woman as well as her celebrity clients. She also hosts private makeup application classes.

About Jaie
Jaie's love for makeup and all things beauty began when around six years old, watching her mother get glammed daily for work or a night out with her dad. Her mom and her beautiful sisters, (all seven of them) are glamorous. Jaie and her cousin would watch them get glammed for a night out and wanted to be and look just like them. Their attention to detail was mesmerizing and she was obsessed! Now, many years later, her love for makeup has never stopped. Williams has an extreme passion for enhancing the beauty that she believes all women; no matter the color of their skin or age, have. She prides herself on being an expert beauty enhancer and skincare expert.

In high school, Jaie studied cosmetology and that is where she found her true calling and love for makeup. Williams also completed a course in permanent makeup at MPressive Faces Academy.

Jaie is a wife and mother of two adult children and has one grandson who is her absolute joy.

Career Highlights

With eight plus years of experience in the makeup artistry industry and along with a plethora of clients, Jaie's career and the network have to give her amazing opportunities and privileges to work with internationally known celebrities, business owners, authors, and a slew of other professionals.

TV/Editorial:

- The Book of John Gray – OWN TV
- Reign Dance Company
- Lakewood Church – Spark Conference
- Our Life TV Show
- Reality Check with the Adolph's

Jaie has several years as a **philanthropist** and **humanitarian** and has served with several organizations to include:

- Project Prom Houston – work with and donated makeup services to underprivileged youth attending prom.
- St. Jude International Gala of Hope and Fashion Show
- Health Fest HCC Eco-Chic Fashion Show
- American Heart Association

Features and Awards Include:

- 2021   Co-Host, Boss Up Houston TV Show
- 2021   Co-Host, The Amber Neal Show (Working Women Wednesday)
- 2021   Reality Check with Adolph's TV Show
- 2019   'Black don't crack' Celebrating ageless women – Defender
- 2019   Our Life TV Makeover Show
- 2019   Small Business Today Magazine
- 2018   Voyage Magazine
- 2018   Rated Bougie MUA of the Year – nominee
- 2018   Houston's 5th Annual Glam Award - Pink Bowl Award Winner

WINNING WOMAN WARRIOR

Delcine Thomas

"EACH MOMENT IS WORTH PUTTING THE EFFORT FORWARD TO PRODUCE RESULTS"

There are sacrifices that we must choose to create a monumental difference in life.

Apostle I.V. Hilliard of New Light Church has often said, "You have to choose to maximize each moment life gives. When we maximize life moments, we have to decide to focus on the task at hand."

I decided to maximize a moment in my life by joining the military. By joining, I knew it would offer me experiences and life-changing adventures.

Women in the military have been the repeated target of debate and controversy for years. Yet, despite it all, I wanted to serve my country. My military journey began while I was living in Baltimore, Maryland. At the age of sixteen, I was trying to decide what I wanted to do at that stage in my life. I knew I wanted to do something different than everyone else. Growing up while in high school, I loved fashion, so I tried my hand at sewing and designing clothes. It was fun but it didn't last. My love for fashion was there, but not sewing.

Once my mother recognized my love for fashion, she helped me enroll in a school of fashion and modeling. At that moment, it was the mark of a new beginning. That was it! I LOVED IT! I loved it because modeling was fun, exciting, and new. I was in training even though it didn't come easily. It took work and determination to embrace this new part of my journey. I graduated from Flair Studio of Dance and Modeling in Baltimore, Maryland.

After graduation, I performed in fashion shows around the country. It gave me a chance to evolve as a winning warrior and become more confident in myself. It also helped change my thinking and how I viewed life. I was modeling all types of clothing from dresses to suits, from casual to dressy, and even swimwear. Attending school along with the fashion shows—helped keep me out of trouble while my mother was at work. Yet I still felt like something was missing.

When I was twenty-seven, being the kind of person that is open-minded, I invited a bold and electrifying decision. Always seeing soldiers in military trucks traveling through the city. A few of us would be so excited when we saw them. I was always waiting for the next time they would come through. One day, I decided to go to the military recruiting office to ask the Army recruiter about signing up. In the military, there are four divisions: Army, Marines, Navy, and Air Force. There are also the Reserves for each branch, which are part-time. After talking to the recruiter, I decided to serve in the Army National Guard. I became adventurous and intrigued by that branch. I had to ask myself if I was ready to take that step before I enlisted and the answer was YES! Despite the many risks, I decided to change my life that day.

On every journey comes a point where there will be a test and our resolve must be to finish. When we exhibit tiredness, fatigue, fear, or pain these moments can test our decisions. When it seems, we do not have the resources to move forward, this can also be a moment that can test our decisions. If we waver, it will weaken our will. That is why we need to be mentally prepared, emotionally grounded, and spiritually armored to pass the tests when they arise.

    I hope that my story will inspire my family, friends, business colleagues, and every reader to push their way in life. To make their goals, dreams, and desires come true. It's never too late. I pray that for each of you that are in my life, those that have inspired me, and for those of you who are getting to know me through this chapter. I am thankful to each of you for being part of my accomplishments. Customer service, project management, and leadership training experience from the military to launch this next venture. Each part of my journey allowed me to learn and expand in so many areas. I am so thankful that I had the opportunity to grow into the winning warrior that I am. I learned discipline, structure, and greater awareness about the importance of taking care of my physical body. Overcoming fears, challenging myself to try new things, and believing in myself, even more, have become my new normal.

ABOUT THE AUTHOR:

Social Media:
IG @lifestyle_cfg
FB @delcine.thomas
Email ddct1808@yahoo.com

Delcine Alexia Thomas is a strong, ambitious, and courageous warrior continuously stepping out in faith while walking through her desert journey. She is a wife, sister, aunt, and business owner. Credit consultant, Imagine your dreams (IYD) Boutique, fashion model. Thomas also adds to her accomplishments, author, motivational speaker, and retired US Army.

Delcine's goal is to inspire every reader that is going through their personal life experience to know, you will make mistakes but GOD will see you through -- by faith!

As a member of the Army National Guard, she has served in Bosnia, Kuwait, and Afghanistan, Iraq. Her military medals and awards include the Army Achievement Medal, Operation Iraq Freedom Medal, National Defense Service Medal, and the NATO Medal.

BALANCE QUEEN

Tiffany Monroe

My life has never been easy or even traditional. The life I now live does not at all reflect the way things started. My beginning provides only a glimpse of how something can start one way and end up different.

You could say I came into the world as an unwanted surprise. My fourteen-year-old mother didn't have much say in what would happen to me after my birth. My grandmother and my great-grandmother decided that my mother would go away to have me and that my great-grandmother's sister would raise me, as her marriage had yielded no children. My great-aunt and great-uncle became my parents and guardians for the next seven and half years.

Although my mother and I saw each other on weekends, I did not live with her until I was eleven years old. The new arrangement took a toll on both of us. My mother provided little maternal affection or nurturing, and I desperately wanted to go back to my godparents.

For much of my childhood, I knew my mother was my mother but didn't understand the life and family pressures she must have faced. Those difficulties pushed her to do things that would keep her in trouble with the police for a while. Some of the decisions she made at that time, both with me and without me, affected our relationship. Most of them, though, she made for survival, out of dependence, and from a desire for independence at such a young age.

By the time my mother and I moved into the same home, she had settled down more and began attempting to step into the full-time role of mother. Although I gave her a chance, I often struggled to let go of the way I had seen her before. As time passed, it became harder to ignore some of my mother's past decisions that came back and haunted our relationship. It led me to decide that I would be different from all I had witnessed.

By high school, part of me had made up my mind that I would leave home for college. This choice came from two factors. First, I desired to get away from my mother's abuse and neglect. Second, I wished to live a life much different from what I had experienced. At age fifteen, I decided I wanted to be a doctor. I worked on my grades, all the while fighting bouts of suicidal thoughts and depression.

I excelled in extracurricular activities that allowed me to flourish. These experiences gave me confidence and reassurance I never found at home. Sports, theater, choir—I got involved in everything I could so I could find the support I did not get from my mother. (In fact, she rarely attended anything I participated in.)

During this time, I decided to be a better mother to my children than my mother ever had been to me. I would always provide the support they needed so they would never have to seek it from other places.

I graduated from high school still intent on becoming a doctor. However, that plan derailed when life happened to me at nineteen years old. In a mentally and sometimes physically abusive relationship, I had my first son. Because my partner wanted me to stay home to raise our child, my aspirations of becoming a doctor quickly faded from my thoughts. When I began to pursue becoming a nurse, my partner destroyed those dreams as well.

As time passed, I realized that continuing my relationship with this man would harm my health and the well-being of my son. So, at a moment's notice, my son and I left to try to start a better life and figure out what to do next.

At age twenty-three, I had a low-paying job and still had no degree. Then life happened again. I had my second son, and within the following year and a half, I found myself the mother of two and not married. Eventually, I did get married. Later, at twenty-eight years old, I decided to go to school to become a professional bridal consultant. This field interested me because I had arranged my wedding and my cousin's to perfection. I enjoyed bridal consulting and began to believe I could do it on the side for extra money. As I worked toward this goal, I also set a goal to receive a degree in business administration.

Difficulties arose with my husband over these aspirations. He made it clear that he did not like the idea of my starting a business or earning a degree. He would say things to deter me from what had now become my dreams. For example, during my studies, I arranged baby showers, wedding showers, and even weddings here and there. My husband started to tell me that I spent too much time on "business stuff" and school. He claimed he didn't understand why I wanted to do any of this anyway.

These statements kept reminding me of my older son's father, and they made me push myself to finish school. But after earning my credentials as a professional bridal consultant, I sat on them for about six years to appease my husband and to spend time with our children (we now had three). I knew I would love running a bridalconsulting business, and I didn't intend to give up on it. It was just not the right time to start.

As time passed, I got my associate's degree and then my bachelor's degree in business. I came up with all types of business ideas but did not follow through on any of them. None gave me the feeling that I had when planning or helping someone with an event.

I found that I had a gift for helping and a wealth of useful, on-point knowledge. I also realized that my eye for things was an asset. Even in unexpected situations, I adapted well.

Although I had a full-time job, people began asking me for help with their events. While I did not always agree to assist, I did enough to show my work. Over time, even more, people asked me to plan events for them. I gained the experience I needed and decided to turn what I had learned into a real business. At long last, I stepped out and got things going for what became I Do × Two Weddings and Events.

All businesses have ups and downs and dry periods, but I give thanks that I still have a passion for this business. I love helping people, creating, developing, and supporting. It seems I have found a way to do what I love, and no one can take it from me or stop me now. It is just me and the great opportunities that continue to come my way.

I have changed so much from the little girl who had no direction. I have evolved from the woman who hesitated to step out and upset those who trampled my dreams. I have become the woman I wanted to be. I love what I do and will not allow anyone to change my mind about my dreams.

This all happened because I made a choice. I chose to not allow my past to control my future. I chose to live a better life than what I was handed. I chose to evolve.

ABOUT THE AUTHOR:
Social Media:
IG @tts_back
FB @tiffany.monroe.520
Email chryar316@gmail.com

Tiffany is a divorced mother of three. She has worked in the oil and gas industry for the last twelve years. She has owned a business since 2010 and currently owns and operates I Do × Two Weddings and Events. Tiffany is also working toward her real estate license. She helps and assists others in every area of her life. She loves God and people.

"You can be who or whatever you want to be; you just have to make a choice."

-Anonymous

The middle of life, it's the eye opener, it's the time when you start realizing what is truly important to you, and what doesn't matter. It is the time when critical circumstances can come and mold you into growing and being aware of who is for and who is against you. It is the time where frivolous things in life wither away. Women in this time, you encounter your "Virtue". You learn your worth… and oooh baby, You're Worth It!!!

The "V" is for Virtue
The Virtue in YOURSELF
The Virtue in PEOPLE
The Virtue in TIME
The Virtue in THE PAST
The Virtue in THE PRESENT
The Virtue in THE FUTURE

The Virtue in FRIENDS
The Virtue in BUSINESS
The Virtue in EDUCATION
The Virtue in FINANCE
The Virtue in your SPOUSE
The Virtue in your FAMILY
The Virtue in LIFE
Virtue-

WOMAN REVEALED

Vanda Smith

Being naive with no vision, hopeful but forgotten, she never gave in. She always knew, deep within, that she wanted more. She would have never overcome the obstacles in her life if she hadn't awoken inside. Looking back on my past, I, Vanda Smith, became a voice for the women who rise through the concrete.

I grew up, isolated and sheltered, on an orchard in the small town of Oroville, California. My life has had its obstacles, but being sound-minded is one of my strongest traits. However, I somehow always get the short end of the stick. I noticed this early in my life which left me feeling unsure of myself, and I looked for love in the wrong places.

My parents' relationship crumbled under the pressures of drug use and long-distance struggles. As a result, my siblings and I got tossed around; moving from place to place in a world and system devoid of compassion. In foster care, I relied on an inner voice to comfort me. As I longed for my parents, I was always consumed with a desire for love.

Eventually, my grandmother took us in. She was slightly disconnected yet very caring, but my siblings and I never healed from this chapter of our lives without our parents. Their absence brought me into a depression that I wasn't aware of until Pastor Adrian, a positive role model of mine, brought it to my attention. He predicted that I would encounter many hardships in my life, and he was right.

I dreamed of having children, but I never wanted to be a single mother. Because of my difficult childhood, I struggled to understand the love which caused my relationship to end in turmoil, and I became a single mother of five children. At that point in my life, I believed that no one would ever truly love me and that life would only be one of suffering in this world.

I needed something real. My desire for love became fulfilled when my father and I reunited after nineteen years apart. The emptiness in my heart could finally start to heal. Our relationship was magical as if we had never separated. I felt secure and seen. Finally, I understood real love. I enjoyed every moment I had with him until he passed away eight years later.

My father's death shook my world. Alone again, I went into a dark depression, and anger consumed my heart. One day, I decided to go to church, and it changed my life forever as I started to do deep shadow work. Surrounded by loving people, I managed to enroll with Counseling and Celebrate Recovery—where I started a twelve-step program. With the help of the church community and counseling, I learned to face my fears and cope with my pain.

My boyfriend—who is now my husband—also helped me to escape my sorrows. We both wanted to break the generational trauma passed down in our bloodlines. Together, we dug deep to heal our bodies, minds, and souls. We realized that our problems had deep roots in the thoughts we had, the foods we ate, and the things we said to ourselves. I finally understood that, all along, it was me who had the power to change my life.

I am completely grateful for the woman that I am today. I am happily married, and I have an amazing family. My mother is now drug-free, and we have formed a wonderful relationship. The pain from my past no longer shames me. Instead, it serves as a reminder of the girl who rose from the concrete.

"Disrespect the hell out of your comfort zone, because growth and amazing things are on the other side waiting for you."
–Vanda Smith

That is my motto.

ABOUT THE AUTHOR:
Social Media:
FB @vanda.smith.73
Email vandalashawn@gmail.com

    Vanda Lashawn Smith was born in San Jose California. At nine years old when she moved to the city of Oroville. Vanda grew up on an orchard full of fruit. Raised by her grandparents whom were very strict she lived sheltered. In 2005, Smith moved to Houston TX to build a relationship with her father. This is where she met her husband of sixteen years and has a blended family of nine kids. Vanda loves living in Texas. She has grown in so many ways and has met the most amazing people there. Smith's life has been a true adventure and it is only the beginning!

A STORM THE WHOLE TIME

iiiYansaje T. Muse

Pataki. Oun Mi Ojo Bi, Okudu Marun, Odun Egbawa Kanlelogun, Merinleadorin Ojo Igba Akoko. **(Translate: Diary. Today is Friday, June 4, 2021. 74 days into Spring Equinox)**

Today brings a day of reflection. I am truly astonished when I sink into Olokun's wealth of my life's memories. They reveal to me how the Eegun (ancestors) and Orisa were speaking to, guiding, chastising, nurturing, and forging me into the woman I am today—long before I knew of them, let alone believed in their existence. They were the keys to the intensities behind my evolution as a woman and a spirit. My scars were sacred, my joys extreme. For me, the breaking points and evolution moments were the same. Evolution is an alluring word that many may use, but the process behind it is a tedious one. A diamond is a seriously evolved coal, but of course, it must first go through the fire, and my volcano is deep. At first, my life seemed to be as a still mountain, collecting wisdom through observation and experience, but when evolution time came, the eruption was massive. To this day, it still is.

In most nature-based faiths, The cycle of life goes as follows: birth, adolescence, coitus, eldership, transition. It is believed when a child is born to the earthly realm, the ancestor realm weeps a loss, as we weep when loved ones in the earthly realm return to their ancestors. Childhood is that space between birth and adolescence. It is a time of wonder, a time where all things are possible. It is a time of untainted innocence and unbridled imagination. As for me, I was forged between Halloween night and Dia de Los Muertos and made my solar return on August 1st. I was born the fourth child of my mother, the seventh of my father. My birth name was and is the first spiritual name I received. I am named for both my maternal and paternal grandmothers, Ivory Louriyne. I am the fourth female child in my lineage to carry my first name. Ivory. A name that means rare and pure...I laugh and scoff in equal measure.

The childhood part of my life was full of pain and wonder in equal measure. I learned the hard way to listen to my first mind, as to do so would be to listen to the voice of the Most High, the Goddess within. I was a curious child with an insatiable thirst for the secrets behind life's curtains. I loved nature more than toys, reading books more than mindless play. I loved to read because it allowed me to place myself in settings of the story in question, as an early form of astral travel! I was into history, art, animals, and most of all, discovery.

When it came to religion, I was confused. Spirit always spoke to me, but I was raised in a religion that considered such things a sin. In my spirit, I always found "God," per se, everywhere BUT the churches I was told He resided in. My developing intuition was oftentimes chalked up to an "overactive imagination," so in the beginning, I didn't take my gifts too seriously in front of others. However, my childhood was filled with second-guessing myself because no one seemed to see the world as I did. I was different but didn't understand how or why, and it often subjected me to ridicule. Sometimes the ridicule came from my very own siblings.

The morals I was given as a child were a crossroads between spoken rules and unspoken influence. I picked up on both, as I was a child who missed nothing. The morals I was given were heavily Christian based, preached far more than practiced.

I was taught things like "turn the other cheek," "be the bigger person...," "what would Jesus do?"

Even then, it felt like grooming. This same grooming makes abusers feel comfortable. It was in this area I felt areas of my foundation cracking. It was at this moment I secretly searched for something to fill these cracks. Even at this tender age, I longed to be close to what I perceived to be "God," but found the very religion I was raised in to be a barrier. Was I a Devil's child? The inner war begins...

In a scholarly sense, I was considered by many to be an above-average student. I was very advanced, wise beyond my years, they'd say. I was a straight-A student, a dancer, I played softball, etc. I even explored my shapeshifting abilities in acting in school plays, feeling different parts of my own spirit under different names. These things were fun, but they still felt on a surface level to me, positive distractions to keep me out of trouble. I had many achievements and much admiration from my teachers. Adults always expected more out of me than others, and I didn't know why. At times, it was a struggle to make friends because I was strange to some, outright hated by others. To me, I was just me. When I turned the lights out at night, I would retreat into my secret, supernatural place. These facts of my early life were but one of many clues in getting acquainted with my ancient essence.

My childhood influences were few because there were people I admired, but it didn't mean I wanted to be like them. I was busy looking for the secrets to understanding Spirit, as well as myself. There was one influence that greatly humored me...in a way that I wouldn't understand until years down the line. I would see her on commercial breaks in between my favorite cartoons (the X-MEN was serious business, by the way. No one could tell me I wasn't Storm!) She was a psychic advisor named Miss Cleo. At the time, I was taught it was sinful to believe in such things, but something about her humored me on a deep level. She humored me to a point where my laugh was more than a laugh. It was a nervous revelation yet to materialize.

My childhood molded my womanhood through reflections in hindsight. Memories of my childhood served as affirmations that the heavens made no mistake the way I was designed. There was nothing wrong with me, despite what I was made to believe. My childhood prepared me to live in the totality of faith, with little desire to be a part of the mundane world. Deep down, I never let the girlish wonder of living be diminished...even to this day.

Adolescence for me was rough. My entire way of life had changed from a suburban city girl to rural country life in a small town. We returned to the hometown of my father's roots. On a good note, I learned to farm, and the presence of ancestral spirits got stronger. Their voices got louder. I began seeing things before they happened, but my religion forbade me to trust myself...such things were a sin, remember? This was the opposite of the vision of my life...as well as those around me. I imagined that I would outgrow my esoteric energies, but they only intensified. I became introverted and extroverted in equal measure and a serious mystery to myself. My father became an ancestor in my adolescence. It was the beginning of a place of inner numbness...depression. I learned to be strong instead of being human, and it proved to be unhealthy. It was learning I would later unlearn.

I was blessed with an outlet, though. In 7th grade, I had an English teacher named Ms. Eloise Turner, who introduced me to poetry. She was a spark that ignited my inner flame, and to this day, I still write poetry to release my innermost thoughts. In poetry, I began to discover a power all my own.

I was extroverted in terms of keeping a long list of achievements; varsity cheerleader, R.O.T.C Corps Commander, drama club, local pageants, and such. Unfortunately, I wasn't just silent anymore out of fear of not making sense to anyone. There were underlying darknesses that challenged my sense of self-worth as a woman. *(See the book "Unmasking the Truth Behind I'm Good" by Dr. Jayco McGowen, Ennun Walker, Kevin Trent, and iiiYansaje T. Muse for the detailed story. Available on Amazon).* Deep inside, I crouched over the light in my soul and vowed to protect it with my life, no matter what price I would pay to keep it. I learned early in life that keeping on the light in your spirit places you at war with the world, and oftentimes, yourself.

I was going to church a lot. The more I went, the less it made sense. I grew wearier of feeling the presence of God everywhere but church. I found it less moral to always turn the other cheek and be the bigger person. By then, I was out of cheeks to turn. Those who were slapping my face got more comfortable, not repentant. I went into a mental and spiritual survival mode. I used my book smarts to land an honor's high school diploma, a couple of scholarships to PVAMU, and my freedom from my adolescent stage of glamorized torment. I was evolving within, and the lava beneath my still mountain was heating up. It seemed I was surrounded by fewer women I wanted to be anything like. It wasn't personal. I just felt like an old spirit trapped in a young body. In the still of late, quiet nights in the country, I could hear the spirit speak clearly. I also took refuge in music, more so than I did as a child. I got a lot more comfortable being in my own little world. God/ess and I understood us.

The full blossom into womanhood was far more enjoyable than the hatching thorn-patch of puberty. However, I faced the biggest challenge in my evolution to date in my young womanhood. My spiritual evolution and explosive rebellion went hand in hand, and I became my own worst enemy. I was achieving on one hand, and self-sabotaging on the other. Because of my spiritual standing, I developed an unhealthy complex with God/ess because I didn't understand my divinity as a woman, as I felt that The Father, The Son, and the Holy Spirit were barren, and left no place for a woman to be truly divine. All the while, my ego was fed to the point of gluttony, and demons were gambling for my soul. My alter began to scare me, and it came clear to me that only one of us could rule.

Despite my frustration and confusion, I chose to be a woman of the Spirit. That choice led to life as I knew it as being over. I'd lost everything and everyone. Life had broken me down to nothing but the light in my soul that I'd been crouched over for so many years. I took a break from life and some time within to cultivate it. I went from a popular college diva to a phantom everybody wondered what happened to...but the most amazing thing happened in the midst of it all. All the spiritual mystery I held within filled the places where all had been lost. This poem can better explain.

I bet you wonder where I've been....
Within.

Absent but perhaps evolving like tsunamis over ocean waves
praises up, abundance rains
she makes the truth plain, and growing pains
more than bearable
unknowingly wearable, minyon scare-able.

I bet you wonder where I've been...
Within.

Transitioning wind velocities into funnel clouds,
proudly destructing structures built on misunderstandings
landing artistic expressions of gratitude in the sky
tapping into 9 past lifetimes I've
been making love to stout truth until the sweat purges the lies
Verses from Akashic records pour out through my pores
shape-shifting in its rawest form
with all doors for meaninglessness closed, locked.
An empty cellar restocked
a ticking time bomb, just watch.
In Olodumare's vintage vineyard of nourishing black grapes
that await to taste
sweeter with time....and authentic wisdom...such a savage peace

unimprisoned at least in an exiled paradise-like Assata
fortunate to escape Sarah Bartman's fate
learning to love the awkward sound of my voice like Nina...to dream of....
Stretching bare on Ogun's blacksmith table and letting God remold
reforge, but of course
Angels call our voices for their reasons
shielded under Orisa wings we comb the globe in new believing
consecrated tongues, new speaking
grieving the old self with no bereaving
receiving the conceiving seeds and leaving
auras of divinity in our wake
like blackeye peas marinating in 4 seasons
just waiting on the cornbread to bake....

I bet you wonder where I've been....
Within.

Rolling.
Twisting lavender incenting thoughts evoked
the expanding spiral spoke
provoked in Mary Jane smoke
when I make my blunts float
spirits speak then vaporize
words and actions synchronize
strategize, execute the rise above low spiritual conditions
switching positions with systematic screw-overs
and climbing back on top of my world
fingers interlocked
Minyons love not knowing Jack drunk, so I let them take their shots
I pray they find truth in my thoughts

I bet you wonder where I've been...
Within.

not hiding under a rock, but something like that
a hermit from conformity, snacking on facts....
Watching, waiting, anxiously anticipating
in a home, I built inside my painting
and a chamber in my soul where someone once blocked my light
now Heaven and Earth consummation in plain sight.
I tossed my Dutch clogs
and took a barefoot jog
down hallways of abandoned rooms in my DNA strands
reignited eternal flames...and it's hot, get a fan
ancestors occupy, sing their songs, I'm a band
dancing to the rhythm of a divine master plan
for that authentic swag in my back when I stand....
To set the records all the way straight.

I bet you wonder where I've been.
Within.

    As you can probably guess, the major point of evolution for me was converting faiths and returning to the ancient traditions of my ancestors. This was three years after my laughter at Miss Cleo brought about its true revelation. Now that she is an ancestor, I can imagine she's laughing at me, now that I have her job. The eruption of the still mountain turned volcano happened Wednesday, October 11, 2017. I was initiated to Ifa Orisa as a Priestess of Oya. I received another spiritual name then: Iyansa Ogbo Funimole, meaning "Ancient Mother of Nine who Brings the Light." That name has since evolved to "Odujinmi Oyabunmi Abimbola," meaning "Awakened by the Odu, A Gift from Oya in Abundance." Remember when I mentioned believing I was Storm of the X-Men as a child? Well, in some regards, I am. Oya is the orisa that rules the cemeteries and the STORMS. My childhood premonition had come full circle. I'm comfortable in all layers of my skin now. God/ess gave it to me, why not?

ABOUT THE AUTHOR:
Social Media:
IG @iiiyansasmotherblu
FB @iiiyansanojlftmuse
Email scribessmuse@gmail.com
Website www.poeticallymused.org

iiiYansaje T. Muse is a Priestess of Oya, (Iya Odujinmi Oyabunmi Funimole Abimbola) is a 7-year professional prophetic counselor, visual artist, poet, radio host, author, and mystic journalist. As a spiritual counselor, iiiYansaje is fluent in over 16 different forms of divination, including astrology, numerology, dream interpretation, obi, six tarot decks, automatic writing, and conjure arts. They all back up her first line of ethereal intuition.

Her performing art focuses on sacred dance, radio, theater, and jazz poetry. She is featured on the Season 1 cast of *"Galactical Goddesses."* In visual art, she is the sole creator of iiiYansa's Glass Gourd, an infinite collection of recycled wine and spirit bottle paintings. With this artistic platform, she creates home and business blessing décor, centerpieces for special events, CUSTOM ORDERS, and themed collections. She is also a radio host with 17 years of experience in public radio.

iiiYansaje's published written works include *"Crying Diamonds: 11 YEARS LATER,"* her firstborn Poetry Collection, *"All Things Aries,"* and *"Memoirs in Waiting,"* the first volume of her mystic arts journal, *"The iiiSangoma"*. The journal's feature article is a grassroots film titled, *"Legba, Christ, and the Crossroads,"* She also has guest articles in *TRE Magazine* (July 2011), *Visit Black Houston Magazine*, and *HOTEP Magazine*. She also has a chapter in the collective book project, *"Unmasking the Truth Behind I'm Good,"* alongside Dr. Jayco McCowan, Ennun Walker, and Kevin Trent.

More of her writings can be found on her upcoming series of blogs, *The Windsong Kraal of Oracles: Mother Blue Hues* (Mondays), *The Peridot Poultice* (Tuesdays), *The Malbec*

Planetarium (Wednesdays), *iiiChings & Scarlet Serenes* (Thursdays), *Honey, Love and Warpaint* (Fridays), *The Jester's Intersection* (Saturdays), *Alabaster Divine* (Sundays), and *Ancestral Legacies for the Ancestors.*

On February 22. 2021, iiiYansaje launched an online radio station, **222.9 The Mothership, Your Mystic Haven on the Airwaves**. It is a radio station that preserves the genius of black music as well as teaches the ways of the mystics. It can be accessed on The 222.9 The Mothership App, or

www.poeticallymused.org/mothership.

iiiYansaje is an HBCU graduate, holding two bachelor's degrees in theatre arts and mass communications media study. She is also a member of Zeta Phi Beta Sorority, Inc. In the future, iiiYansaje aspires to continue to create a large, stout body of creative work that heals, enlightens, entertains and inspires others...all because she believes that the highest form of spiritual healing is creative expression.

For more information, visit www.poeticallymused.org

Favorite Quote:

"Everybody thought Noah was crazy until it started to rain."
– *iiiYansaje T. Muse*

WOMAN WARRIOR

Cadori

As a child, I was raised in a very strict religious-based family. I am one of thirteen siblings and I am the oldest girl. This meant that I was basically the first girl to have to go through all of the testings on everything from learning how to cook, how to properly clean the house to dating. But the dating part was a big 'No' for me. Because I was the oldest girl and my daddy was very strict and old fashion as they used to call it. He didn't want me dating until I was almost out of high school. So that just meant I had to sneak around and talk to boys. The strict dating rules along with other strict rules like, not being able to hang out with classmates and go to the mall or the skating rink and so on meant that I had to sign up for school activities just to have something that resembled a social life. I and my oldest brother were the built-in babysitters or as I would call it, the miniature parents. We were left to take care of our siblings more times than I can remember.

I believe that my strict upbringing made it harder for me to discern the different types of people that were in the world and this led me to be a people pleaser most of my life and also being very trusting of people who didn't have my best intentions in mind.

As I entered my teenage years I began to develop low self-esteem. As I look back now I know that it derived from the fact that I just didn't feel like I fit in most of the time. Even though I was involved in different school activities like the band, the choir, the volleyball team. The feelings of low self-esteem were primarily because outside of the school activities, I didn't have much of a social life. When most of the girls my age were hanging out with our friends and going to the movies, the mall, and the after-school events, I wasn't allowed to go. I missed those types of bonding experiences which made me feel left out when conversations were going on. As time went on in height school I just got used to not hanging out with friends and the low self-esteem wasn't as bad as it used to be. And a positive side of being left out was that I didn't feel like I needed other people's opinions on things.

And because I didn't know what it felt like to value a friend's opinion, I didn't miss it. That gave me a little bit of an advantage as far as looking at things differently than the crowd so to speak. As a teenager, you think you know what's best but most times you don't. And while I would have rather been able to hang out with friends, overall, the best learning outcome was me navigating a lot of things in my life by myself. Though sometimes those experiences were painful, I did learn some life lessons. I was still able to participate in various activities in high school of which a few were, the DECA (Distributive Education Clubs of America), Marching Band, Majorette, the Beauty Pageant where I placed proudly as the 3rd runner up!

I also came up with the idea and formed a new PEP Club at my high school with the help of my DECA teacher. This was the first one I'm the history of the school.

After I graduated high school I got married and started a family. I also enrolled in college but the financial challenges of having a child and bills combined with a nonsupporting husband did not permit me to finish.

I had to grow up super-fast in the new role as a mother and a wife! This was not what I was truly ready for but I gave it my best. For certain, I knew how to take care of a child because I helped to raise most of my siblings. But the marriage thing was a whole different level. And after five years of marriage, three children, and a cheating husband—I ended up filing for a divorce. Continuing to live with someone who was not only cheating but was also verbally and physically abusive at times—was not an option. That marriage took more of my time than I should have allowed—but I held on. But because my parents never getting a divorce and my mama tolerating some things from my daddy, it made me tolerate some things that I should not have put up with. And those marriage vows, particularly the "for better or worse" part also made me keep trying when I should have been running out of that marriage.

The divorce became final after six long years of marriage. But what I didn't know at the time was that I needed to be alone for a while to heal those hurtful wounds from that marriage before entering a new relationship. Because of the hurt feelings and rejection, I started a new relationship before my divorce was official. I met a nice man at my job who gave me all the things that my ex did not. So, we moved to another state together, and after my divorce, we got married. Now, I found myself in a new marriage with my three small children and my new husband (he had no children). Shortly after we were married, I found out that my new husband had an abusive side to him as well—especially when it came to disciplining our children. I later found out that he didn't have the best relationship with his biological dad, who lived in the house with him as a child. My new husband's mother told me on a couple of occasions that his dad physically and verbally disciplined him in front of his friends a few times during his upbringing. Eventually, I had to enforce a 'no physical discipline' policy for my new husband after the birth of our two children.

This caused many problems in our marriage over the years, in addition to his lying, cheating, and verbal and physical abuse. But because of my desire to not fail at a second marriage, and always worrying about what other people would say—I kept trying. Not wanting to deal with the second set of children being upset with me for divorcing their dad, my low self-esteem, and not wanting to be alone—I tolerated way more than I ever should have with him. I allowed the good things that he did to overshadow the bad. While I was able to finish my Nursing Degree in this marriage, there was too much mental abuse ongoing for me to remain married to him. I filed for a divorce after a twenty-four-year marriage to what turned out to be a narcissist. After I got out of that marriage and started getting mental health therapy, I started valuing myself more. Then I began researching his behavior.

I concluded that he was a narcissist. I had to forgive myself which was the hardest thing for me to do. I remember my therapist telling me something that helped me to forgive myself.

She said, "Well Cathy you don't have a crystal ball and you can't read someone else's mind. If your husband is telling you something and you have no proof that he is lying then you only did what any trusting spouse would do and that is to believe him. You can't blame yourself for what you didn't know. So, give yourself a break for not knowing."

Now I feel free from the mental abuse and I invest in my happiness. As a result, I can truly say that I love myself from the inside out! Now I fill my cup up all the time before I pour it into anyone else. These are the things I had never done before.

I have recently started two new businesses, of which one is an "I LOVE ME" clothing line with t-shirts and hoodies. I've also written a #1 Amazon best-selling book titled, *Ladies Love Yourselves First, That's Happiness.*

I have two favorite quotes created by me:
"There's only one you on the planet, so be yourself because no one else can be you!" - CaDori

"An original is always worth more than a copy—so be yourself" - CaDori

ABOUT THE AUTHOR:
Social Media:
IG @cadoribrand
FB @cadoribrand
Website Address https://cadori.net/
Email cadoribrand@gmail.com

Cathy Marshall was born in Birmingham, Alabama. The eldest girl of thirteen children, she is a natural-born leader. Known as CaDori, she coined the name as a combination of her name, her mother Doris, and her late son Dougie.

CaDori loves helping others. She is the mother of five and is a registered nurse. She spends a tremendous amount of time giving back to her community. Before becoming a nurse, she was once homeless, jobless, and lived in a shelter. Her children were very young, and she experienced first-hand the struggle of depending on good-hearted people and her faith in God. CaDori wanted to help others in need. In 2017, she founded a nonprofit charity, CaDori Helping Hands, Inc. She donated baby supplies to young mothers and delivered cleaning and personal care items to families who lost everything during Hurricane Harvey. She also donated backpacks full of school supplies to children in a local shelter and fed over 100 people displaced by the hurricane at a hotel in Livingston, Texas. In 2018, CaDori Helping Hands, Inc. provided turkeys and hams for Thanksgiving and gave away winter coats to those in need.

In addition to CaDori Helping Hands Inc., CaDori also founded Dougie's Kids, Inc., a charitable organization dedicated to helping and ensuring the well-being of children across America. It's named after her oldest son, Bobby Denerio Marshall Brown, affectionately known as "Dougie," who passed away in 2010 in a motorcycle accident. Dougie adored children and gave helpful advice, mentored, took them to fun places, and supported them by attending games. To date, Dougie's Kids has donated funds to shelters, schools, and awarded scholarships which have positively impacted the lives of many children.

As an entrepreneur, CaDori's "I Love Me" apparel, CaDori Helping Hands Inc. merchandise, as well as her print books are available for sale on her website: Cadori.net and on Amazon.com. After the release of CaDori's first book, *Women Put Yourselves First and Be Happier*, and then a cookbook, her positive impact became evident. She had a fierce momentum with tons of media exposure within a couple of months. CaDori has been featured in several articles and on numerous radio shows, in An Interrupted Blogs article, an eTrade Wire article, on HousontTXBlack.com, in Urban Grandstand Magazine, Plaid For Women Dallas, Kontrol Magazine, Melan Magazine, U.S. Reporter, Can We Talk Source Radio with Myra McKnight, The Ladiez Room Radio in Birmingham with Clarissa, The Covert Report with Susan Lindauer, Shadow Politics Talk Show with Senator Michael Brown and Maria Sanchez, and Bob Burns in Your Afternoon Talk Radio Show. CaDori is also a radio co-host on the all-new Amber Neal radio show on 953jamz.com Houston on Wednesdays, for The Working Women Wednesdays segment from 2-4 p.m. She was honored as a Top 10 Philanthropist in Houston, Texas on November 11, 2020, by Amber Neal on Amber Neal Day in the City of Houston. She was also a panelist at the State of The Black Woman Panel Discussion in San Antonio, Texas.

CaDori has a powerful new inspirational book for women which was recently released in November of 2020 entitled, *Ladies, Love Yourselves First, That's Happiness*. Orders are being taken now on her website cadori.net. She has several upcoming virtual events planned for this year and would like to continue making a positive impact in the lives of others, especially during these uncertain times in the pandemic. Recently, CaDori purchased a new van to deliver food and needed household supplies to people in need. CaDori Helping Hands, Inc. gave away 100 laptop computers to children who are economically challenged on September 1, 2020. National Suicide Prevention Week was from September 6-12, 2020. CaDori supported suicide prevention by educating the public on its importance. During October, the charity assisted women in need of mammograms through The Rose in Houston, Texas. CaDori Helping Hands, Inc. raised over $1200 for The Rose breast cancer organization to help fight breast cancer through the sales of her "I LOVE ME" hoodie clothing line at ilovemehoodie.com, with their goal being $2500. CaDori also hosted a turkey and ham giveaway on Thanksgiving, and she will close out the year with her annual winter coat drive for people in need.

    Recently, CaDori had two virtual book talks with a panel of women discussing her new inspirational book for women, which will soon be available on all social media platforms and YouTube. This coming spring, she will have her first charity walk to raise money for victims of domestic violence, with a goal of at least $10K. Depending upon the pandemic and social distance guidelines, CaDori plans on having a ten-city book tour in 2021 as well. She plans on making 2021 a great year for many through her charitable efforts.

RISING PHOENIX

LaShawn Watson

When I found myself kidnapped in a trunk, begging and praying for my life, I had never imagined that something so horrific could happen to me. For the thirty-eight minutes that I was in the trunk, the only thing on my mind was my niece. You may think that surviving this nightmare would inspire me to turn my life around, but I only fell deeper into despair.

Let me start from the beginning. I was a child of a teen mom, and my grandparents were majorly involved in my life. My grandmother devoted herself to prayer. She gave me a foundation of Christian morals and unconditional love like no other. My mom taught me about hard work, from rebuilding trucks to being a star basketball player. I have a little brother, and we became a close duo even though he is eight years younger than me. I wouldn't change my family for the world. The combination of positivity and dysfunction made me who I am today.

I thought my life was meant to go in a direction of fast-paced talking and the gift of gab. With the exception of my grandmother's serenity, my household overflowed with chaos, until a shining star came along. My niece was born in 1999, and the world seemed to be spinning in the right direction. Then, the turmoil began again.

I discovered that I was unable to have a child of my own. What's a girl to do when she's married and wants a child but can't have one? I felt like a failure as a woman, and I couldn't believe what was happening to me.

My life started to spiral, and I had lost the morals that I learned as a child. Soon after learning about my infertility, my grandmother died, and I died along with her. My life had taken a huge leap from the path that I had planned. I lost my values, my husband, and my family. There I was in a new city with new people living the life that I dreaded: a fast-paced one. I worked as a cabaret dancer and endured everything that came with it.

I ventured so far into the drug world that I found myself in some legal trouble. I spent two days in jail, which scared me so much that I swore I would never end up there again. As I awaited trial, I took a call that changed my life forever.

After getting off of the phone, two individuals picked me up, and as soon as I closed the car door, I got the feeling that this ride would ruin me. As this sensation flooded my body, I tried to escape the car, and the driver assured me that he would stop. He told the truth, but the stop did not save me. In a quick motion, he opened the door and pointed a gun at my head. I pushed it away, and he told me that this was not a game.

A thousand thoughts flooded my mind, but the only one I can recall was to keep pushing the gun away from my head. He told me to undress in the middle of the street, and then he sexually assaulted me. Afterward, he forced me into the trunk. I tried to fight it but didn't succeed.

Riding in the trunk, I was naked and scared to death. In an attempt to cope, I began praying and praying louder. I thought of my grandmother and how she didn't raise me to fall into a life like this. I thought of my niece and how she would discover that her aunt died this way. My prayers seemed to echo throughout the car. The driver turned the radio up, but my prayer got louder.

Then, I remembered what my mother had taught me about working on cars. I started pulling the wires on one side of the trunk and pushed my back up against the top of it. The trunk started to open a little when the unthinkable happened. The middle seat opened from the inside, and I thought my heart would beat out of my chest. Knowing that my captors would soon notice my efforts to escape, I would have only one opportunity to free myself, and it had to be quick.

I moved to the opposite side of the trunk, found the pin, and popped the lid open. By pushing my back against the lid, I was able to open it. Tasting freedom, I leaped, tucked, and rolled down the busy interstate. Thanks to the grace of God, there were no other cars on the road that night. Because of my momentum, I rolled for half a mile before I could gain my posture and get up. I lost forty-seven percent of my skin and part of my heel, and I had third-degree burns. It was a nightmare, the scariest experience of my life.

My injuries were so severe that I had to learn to walk all over again. You may think that this horrific experience would be a wake-up call and that it would push me to turn my life around. That didn't happen. I spiraled. Instead of networking drug addicts as I had in the past, I was now the user myself. The courts delayed my previous case because I was a state witness for the kidnapping. After the trial was over and the offender's sentence was forty years, my case was back on the roster. I evaded the trial and had a blue warrant with a felony sitting on my head. As a homeless fugitive, I lived wherever I could network the best deal.

When the helicopters and police surrounded my homestead, I moved back to Houston. Knowing that they wouldn't come back so soon, it was the best place to be. After staying there for six months, the most unexpected thing happened. I was pregnant. Wait, what? I said the same thing. God knows exactly what to do when it's needed most.

I hated myself and the position that I was in as a pregnant addict. Why Lord? To certify my pregnancy, I had an ultrasound, and they gave me a picture of my baby. It was a girl. God gave me the one thing I had asked for long ago: a mini-me.

All the odds were against me. The reality of my situation sunk in two weeks before she was born. I prayed, and I mean genuinely prayed. I didn't even know I could cry out like that. That's the day I began my personal relationship with God.

I promised Him that, if he would heal my baby, I would follow Him. At that moment, I could feel his arms wrapped around us. Thinking about it now still gives me chills. She finally came after I had carried her for ten months and a week. I know nine months is supposed to seal the deal, but I believe that He was waiting on me to cry out to Him. They tested her twice for drugs in her system. The first results came back as positive. With a second test, she was negative. Thank God!

My journey as a mother hasn't been easy, but I've taken it one step at a time. I started by going to rehab for mothers, and I learned how to be a parent.

On my second day there, the counselor made a statement that I still carry with me today: "you may not be responsible for getting down, but you are responsible for getting up."

As the program progressed, another counselor told me that, if I went back to the life I was living, I would die. She called it healthy fear. Well, she got my attention. That is not the life I wanted for my baby. When the program ended after ninety days, I signed up for extended out-patient care, and I found a haven in my church home.

New Jerusalem MBC, Garden City welcomed me with open arms. From day one, they never made me feel ashamed. My daughter and I needed love and biblical guidance, and the church gave it to us. Pastor Jackson wanted partners in the ministry. Partners are the ones that are there for the cause, no matter the circumstances. They stand when no one else will. I felt as though being a partner was my calling, so I devoted myself to the church.

Now that I was home, serving the church, and parenting, I knew that it was time to face the music. Remember, I still had a blue warrant on my head. My church family fasted and prayed with me for days before I turned myself in. They drove me to Austin to stand before the judge.

My experience that day solidified my unyielding faith in God and His eternal love. The judge told me that they had prepared for my arrival and that the papers sentenced me to fifteen months state jail time. My case dropped to a misdemeanor, and I know that there is no other explanation for this miracle except for the mercy of God. Though I had arrived dressed in my whites, prepared to kiss my baby goodbye, I was now traveling home with her by my side.

Now that the weight of my legal troubles had lifted off of my shoulders, it was time to start my life again. When you've been in the drug world, most things disappear or expire, so I needed a driver's license and a social security card. As I worked to pull my life back together, I decided to go to the doctor for a check-up. That's when a new obstacle presented itself to me. I received a diagnosis of sarcoidosis. Just as I was about to beat the storm, a tsunami hit.

The doctors told me that there is no known cure for sarcoidosis and that they don't know how it develops. They put me on medication and steroids, and I had regular doctor's appointments. My face was so full of granulomas—small areas of inflammation—that I didn't recognize myself. I tried to cover them with makeup and failed.

Several months passed. Then, at a WOW (Women of Workmanship) meeting, the moment of truth came. Paul's words about the thorn in his side resonated with me:

"Because of the extravagance of those revelations, and so I wouldn't get a big head, I was given the gift of a handicap to keep me in constant touch with my limitations. Satan's angel did his best to get me down; what he did was push me to my knees. No danger then of walking around high and mighty! At first, I didn't think of it as a gift and begged God to remove it. Three times I did

that, and then he told me, My grace is enough; it's all you need. My strength comes into its own in your weakness." (2 Corinthians 12:7-9, MSG).

ABOUT THE AUTHOR:

Social Media:
IG @lashawn.watson @houstonangelsnutritionllc
FB @lashawn.watson @houstonangelsnutrition
Website Address https://lashawnwatson.goherbalife.com/
Email mrslswh@gmail.com

LaShawn Watson is a single mom, recovery coach, health coach, online business mentor, and business owner of a brick & mortar - Houston Angels' Nutrition, LLC. In this role, LaShawn leads a team providing nutrition, fitness, and all aspects of inspiration, hope, and transformation physically, mentally, and spiritually.

A big believer in recovery, Watson supports the recovery movement and speaks transparency. She celebrates twelve years of recovery and helps her community by using speaking engagements and conferences to give families hope.

LaShawn has a purpose in using her platform to show others the possibility of being a business owner and living a happier healthier lifestyle. Working with Boss Up Houston Network and Black Service Chamber are some of the highlights, but the greatest accomplishment is working alongside her twelve-year-old daughter, Daisy.

DEBORAH

Tricia Kyle

As a child, I learned one thing that has carried me through my life: prayer. And the woman who taught me to pray was my beloved grandmother, the most influential woman to me. Even though our time with one another ended too soon, she had a monumental impact on my life. While she taught me my ABCs, she simultaneously taught me how to pray.

My grandmother taught me to give thanks: "God is great. God is good. Let us thank Him for our food. By His hands, we are fed. Thank You for our daily bread."

She taught me to inquire of the Lord our God: "Now I lay me down to sleep; I pray the Lord my soul to keep. If I should die before I wake, I pray the Lord my soul to take."

And she taught me to always think about and pray (intercede) for others: "God bless..." followed by name after name until I didn't know anymore and began to call out categories. We prayed for those who were sick, hungry, scared, lonely, hurting, or mourning; all the children; mothers, and fathers; and everyone in need. By the time we finished each night, my grandmother had taught me to pray for everyone around the world.

For the short time that Grandmother had me and I had her, she taught me to talk to my Father. This practice has kept me grounded, hopeful, and steady all these years.

My story is a harsh one. It seems almost impossible that all these events could happen to one person. It feels like a Lifetime movie. But if my life shows anything, it shows God's hand of protection and keeping power. Hopefully, that reminds people that God has them throughout all they endure. We have not been forgotten. That's God's amazing grace.

My life was filled with sexual, physical, and emotional abuse. I was prostituted as a toddler, used as a sacrifice, and defiled by many in occult practices for years. On occasion, I was drugged so I would cooperate. I was molested for years by a family member, a man who lived in our home and passed me around to his friends as favors until I was eleven.

I was severely physically abused, and when I was fifteen, my mother told me how she would murder me. She bragged about how no court, no jury, and no judge would convict her. After all, who would convict a wealthy, grieving White mother—a pillar of the community, an entrepreneur, the wife of a senior vice president for a major medical electronics company, and a woman who could cry on cue? However, she wasn't going to do it before her trip. For a year, she and my father had planned for a month-long tour of Europe, and nothing would interfere, not even me. So, they sent me to a shelter, not a friend's house.

One night a few weeks later, I heard that my parents had returned from their trip and would pick me up in two days. I decided to run to save my life. I had not forgotten what my mother had said she would do to me. The night before I left, a fourteen-year-old girl at the shelter befriended me. She said she would run away with me and take me to someone who would take care of us. Despite what I had been through, my still-naïve mind didn't question it.

That next day, as I left, that girl sex trafficked me to a thirty-two-year-old Colombian drug dealer. Unlike my previous abusers, he kept me for his personal use instead of passing me around. I got away from him after a couple of years, but only because he went to prison in another state for drug possession. I then became homeless for years, living in shelters.

I worked hard and focused on bettering my life. Then I walked into a thirteen-year relationship full of domestic violence. I had no rights to my money, my children, or my body. I was raped nearly every day of my life. I became suicidal. I struggled with depression, anger, and loneliness but did my best to function.

Miraculously, I finally broke free from that relationship, though the man still stalked and threatened me for years. Years later, I got into another abusive relationship with a man who I thought offered love and safety. That, too, ran its course, and I learned the value of time alone and healing.

All these things took a toll on a woman who had no self-esteem or self-worth, who felt devalued and of no importance. I have had to work hard to gain a sense of self-confidence, normalcy, and safety so I could heal the wounds that ran deep. Acute trauma, compound trauma, and complex trauma had all affected my life.

Yet I'm here. For the hardest times in my life, prayer became my lifeline. I talked to God, no longer sounding like a children's rhyming book but like a woman pouring out her heart to her Father, the only One present for every event in her life. He witnessed every tear, every time I wanted to die, and even prayed for death because life hurt too much.

God never missed a moment of it and never turned His back. But He also gave me the strength to keep going and to believe. God stayed my hand when I was literally ready to pull the trigger. I prayed at that moment, too: "If You don't mean for me to do this, then You'd better stop me!" He did just that.

I have witnessed miracle after miracle and have seen God's hand of protection too many times to count. He has saved me from so many dangers. God kept me from things like drugs and alcohol, which so many people turn to, to cope with the pain of their lives. He kept me sane and somehow restored everything that others had stolen from me. My joy, my peace, my song, my voice—they are mine because He gave them to me.

My prayers, although quiet in my youth, have grown in strength, faith, and power. But my time in prayer does not always involve me speaking. As time goes on, I spend more time listening and patiently waiting to hear from God. Communion comes from that closeness in which both parties pour out their hearts. It's when we exchange thoughts and feelings: I pour out my heart, and I wait for Him to pour out His heart. That's it. Communion happens when we have confidence in who God is and who we are to God. We are His beloved, and He is our Father.

I saw many influential and strong women while growing up. Unfortunately, when people showed love or concern for me, others either removed me from their influence or pushed me away. It hurt because I've always wanted to feel a sense of belonging. No one, apart from God, had the chance to anchor me in the bedrock wisdom that would have gotten me through life more easily.

I have often questioned why I have had to stand alone for most of my life. It seems that through the scariest, most unsure, and fearful times in my life, it's been just God and me. He wanted me to depend on Him and seek out His will for my life, not someone else's idea of who they think I am. It's taught me to rely on God to lead me, cover me, protect me, counsel me, and provide for me. I have listened intently to human counsel, what people thought was best for me. Although I believe that most of them meant well, they didn't always give God-led or God-inspired advice. They had limited perspectives and didn't know what God had told me. How can someone define you if they didn't create and design you?

Because I so often struggled alone, I didn't feel as if I deserved someone fighting for me. But then I realized I do. God fought for me and won.

When I learned I needed to select a spiritual name for this project, I heard the Lord clearly say what I should choose: Deborah.

Deborah, a wise prophetess and a judge of Israel, discerned the voice of the Lord correctly and brought her people to victory. When she heard the voice of the Lord, she moved. No matter what, she moved because she believed.

If I were to leave you with words of wisdom, the first one would be that you will never go wrong if you follow the leading of God. Proverbs 3:5–6 comes to mind, "Trust in the Lord with all your heart, and lean not on your own understanding; In all your ways acknowledge Him [seek His will, submit], and He shall direct your paths" (NKJV).

The second word of wisdom I would give you comes from Mother Pearl Deaver: "Do today what you can live with tomorrow."

And the third word of wisdom is this: You are not an accident. You were meant to be here. God has a plan and a purpose for your life. And because you are still here, it means that He kept you and your work is not done. Plain and simple. It ain't over.

ABOUT THE AUTHOR:
Social Media:
IG @triciakyle_tk
FB @Tricia-TK-Kyle @tricia.kyle.Ministries
Website Address https://sites.google.com/view/tricia-kyle-ministries/home
Email triciakyleministries@gmail.com

Tricia has five beautifully gifted children and two amazing grandchildren. In her professional life, she wears many hats: businesswoman, gospel singer, songwriter, blogger, vlogger, advocate, mentor, podcast host and creator, teacher, preacher, speaker, author, and ordained minister of the gospel. But if she put all those amazing titles in a nice little box and put a beautiful bow on it, that bow would be named Servant.

Someone once asked Tricia, "What do you most want to be remembered for?" Only two things came to mind. The first one was her love for God. Tricia wants her love for God to be evident, real, and tangible. Not because she attends church or because she wears a cross around her neck seven days a week. Not even because she has some bumper sticker or T-shirt declaring her affection for Him. Tricia wants her love for God to be so evident that you can see it in the way she walks, talks and lives life—not for show but for real. She wants it to be real for someone who struggles with the question "Is God real?" or "Does God love me?"

The second thing Tricia wants to be remembered for is her love for people. She wants to be remembered as someone who genuinely has a heart for God and people (not just God's people). This world can be a cold place, and we as individuals may not have a huge sphere of influence. But the people that we cross paths with ought to feel our love for God and each other. Otherwise, Tricia says, what are we doing?

AMEREPIPHANY

Chimere Bacon-Destin

I was born different, beautiful, and uniquely crafted. Some things have happened in my life that I can honestly say I went through because only I could handle them. Since turning a certain age, I also have realized that every memorable moment has prepared me for and propelled me to the next. I can look back on specific instances now and fully comprehend them, even though I didn't understand them at the time. Whatever we might call this ability, I have had it since birth. Yes, birth—the day I was blessed to come down and be a blessing to this world.

Let's start from the beginning. After all, we can't possibly understand the story of a person's evolution without the beginning.

In the Beginning

As a child, I remember waking up to the good smells of pancakes, eggs, bacon, sausage, and Folgers coffee. I was everybody's baby: the only child of my mom and the only grandchild of my grandparents until about age thirteen. I've always been an old soul and more mature than most. My mom, a hardworking single parent, passed on her work ethic to me. My grandmother was an entrepreneur (a beautician) and a true missionary. These two made for a tough act to follow, but strong women have always surrounded me. They taught me to have the qualities of a strong woman.

For example, one incident from my childhood stuck with me and still rings in the back of my mind. I saw my grandmother work diligently for many things for her church. Everything that she took part in, she gave 100 percent of her time and effort. This incident showed me that betrayal can and will happen among the ones you know best. I didn't know it at the time, but it prepared me for my life's journey. When betrayal arrived at my doorstep, my mind instantly went back to that specific moment, and I saw my grandmother. Gracefully broken, strong-willed, and stern, she unapologetically spoke her piece without using choice words or elevating her voice. But the words she spoke stuck and affected everyone in the room. Within the next few weeks, she became president and received awards.

That experience taught my younger self what my older self would need in similar moments. It taught me to always be my genuine self, even when people don't receive it.

"I ain't for everybody" and "Everybody can't handle my anointing."
– Chimere Destin

Growing up, I did not do a lot of deviating. I was popular, and I wanted to experience everything. My mom was a cool parent, but she had her own style of parenting. I was an honor-roll student, and I didn't have any disciplinary problems.

I did have a problem with some adults; I must say this. Children should respect their elders, but sometimes adults should hear children out instead of quickly dismissing them. I'll give two examples from my life. These incidents helped mold me into someone who speaks out and does not let anyone, even people in authority, run over me.

The first event took place when I was a cheerleader in middle school. Our cheer coach had a problem with me, mainly because I had more influence over my teammates than she did. We went to cheer camp one year. I didn't feel good by the time my three roommates and I got to our hotel room. I got in bed and went to sleep early. The other girls stayed up, ordered pizza, and made a mess. The coach came into our room, woke me up, and told me to get out of bed and throw the trash away. None of my roommates pointed out that I hadn't eaten anything or that I had gone to bed before they had started eating.

At the time, I didn't say anything. Instead, I told my mom what had happened, and she handled it the next day. After the camp, I quit the cheer squad and got onto the dance team immediately. Now the coach claimed I had wanted to do that all along. I could have said something to contradict her statement. Instead, I kept moving.

In this situation, my "friends" stood by and let me take the rap for something I had nothing to do with. Through this experience, I learned how to handle them from that point on.

The second incident involved my first experience of racism. I attribute my exposure to diversity to my mom. She has wanted and will always want the best for me. She took me out of "hood" schools and moved us to the suburbs. In high school, I went to a truly diverse institution. I believe it had every ethnicity represented among the students. The teachers? Not so much.

This became a problem when auditions came around for the first play of the school year. I had participated in theater since kindergarten. I had starred in plays, sung, danced, and won University Interscholastic League (UIL) division competitions and other awards. Of course, I wanted to continue my theater participation in high school.

At the audition, I tried out for a few roles and received a standing ovation from my peers. However, the theater teacher, a White male, smized at me from his desk. The results came in, and I was the understudy for every role. "What?" you might say. Yes, I hadn't believed that could happen, either. Of course, I passed on any involvement in the play, and a few of my more cooperative friends got parts.

Unfortunately, this man also taught theater classes for all grades. Later in the year, during class, he wrote up one of my friends. Suspicious, I asked to see the write-up. This turned into me getting written up and my request for removal from the theater class. So, I created my own lane to drive in. My friends and I spent a lot of time building up the school's African American Heritage Group that first year. Still, I had sacrificed my love for theater and maybe even a scholarship for peace. (Luckily, I picked theater back up in college.)

Through this experience, I learned that some circumstances will not change, no matter how right you are.

"You have to learn to recognize the game, play the game, and beat them at their own game."

–Chimere Destin

As I grew into adulthood, I saw the world for what it was. I have always been a "woke" individual. I don't live in alternate realities. It is what it is with me. I'm not and never want to be a poster child for anything. Yes, I've been molested, abused, homeless, and betrayed. Yes, I've experienced life-and-death situations. But none of that defines me. I have a story of survival, and I don't want to dwell on the things I've survived. I've told those stories. I want to focus on how I evolved.

Healing comes with (1) the acknowledgment that something happened, (2) the acknowledgment of your part in it, (3) the acknowledgment of the actions of the other party, and (4) the resolution. Too many times, we look to play the victim (because we are the victim), but we should focus on moving to victory. How do we get past our issues if we make those issues more important than moving beyond them?

Evolution starts here when you can say to yourself, "I no longer accept this in my life." When you take the steps to remove a harmful person, place, or thing from your life—at that moment, you become unapologetically you.

I don't care if you don't like it. I don't care how you feel about me. My happiness comes from making myself happy. So, I had to get uncomfortable in those conversations that needed to happen because the only true evolution comes from a change in you. How can you be different and the same at the same time? You can't. It's impossible.

Why Do We Evolve?

I've said it many times, and I say it to my coaching clients: We evolve because a change needs to happen for us to move to our next level. We evolve because the people we are today cannot go into a higher vein while staying the same. We evolve because when evolution takes place, we peel away layers.

The past is the past. While those memories still exist, they should be footprints that stay behind as we continue. I cannot look back; I must keep moving forward. The people that we leave behind were meant for that season, and seasons do change.

Evolution took place for me because I now have full control of who I am as a woman. I know what I want and how those things feel. I know what I don't want. I know through experience and circumstance that compromise comes at a price. I no longer compromise for the happiness of others. I've given too much of myself too many times before.

So, I evolve to live as the truest version of me. I evolve to give the best of me to my children. I evolve to fully develop the gifts that God has provided. I evolve to provide true love to my spouse. I evolve to fulfill the destiny set for my life. I evolve in purpose, through purpose, and on purpose.

ABOUT THE AUTHOR:

For Chimere's full biography, see the About the Lead Author section at the end of this book

O

Omega is the 24th and final letter in the Greek alphabet. The word literally means "great O" (*ō mega*, mega meaning great.)

As the final letter in the Greek alphabet, omega is often used to denote the last, the end, or the ultimate limit of a set, in contrast to alpha, the first letter of the Greek alphabet; see <u>Alpha and Omega</u>. (Wikipedia)

The lasting legacy you leave, after your story is told, what will people say about you after you have left this earth. What lasting impression do you leave with people when you leave the room. If you have yet to figure it out, you should start living your life on purpose. The purpose to leave impression in this world on people, not to impress, not to prove, but for the better of the greater good.

The "O" is for OMEGA

Your final chapter is simply that your story continues to be great from generation to generation through your Legacy!!!

MEET THE REAL HOUSEWIVES OF HOUSTON

www.therealhousewivesofhouston.org

ABOUT THE LEAD AUTHOR

Chimere Bacon-Destin grew up in Houston, Texas, in a single-parent home. The women in her life have had the greatest influence on her. They have given and shown strength, courage, stability, and success.

After graduating from high school, Chimere earned a bachelor's degree in communications and a master's degree in business administration. While working as a manager and pursuing her goals, she saw a lack of support for and unity among women in business. This situation gave birth to her mission. Striving to stay motivated and positive, Chimere became the founder and CEO of the Real Housewives of Houston Organization. The organization seeks to uplift, inspire, encourage, and aid women in achieving success. Their slogan is "Where success is the reality."

Chimere also works as the CEO and owner of Boss Up Houston Network. This television network provides a platform for small businesses, entrepreneurs, and ministries to cultivate their crafts through broadcasting. She firmly believes in legacy, wealth, and multiple streams of income.

In eastern Nigeria, chi means "God" and mere means "made." In French, chimère means "a dream you cannot touch." With all these elements together, Chimere's name means "God made a dream you cannot touch." She is covered! Her growth and success prove that next-level praise, next-level worship, and immeasurable inheritance have no limits.

Social Media:
IG @mrsbaconbaby_rhwoh @bossuphouston
FB @mrscbacon @bossuphoutx @rhwoh
Website Address www.therealhousewivesofhouston.org
Email rhwohinfo@gmail.com

www.ingramcontent.com/pod-product-compliance
Lightning Source LLC
Chambersburg PA
CBHW051706160426
43209CB00004B/1035